Out *of* Darkness

into the Light

JUDITH WALTERS

WESTBOW
PRESS®
A DIVISION OF THOMAS NELSON
& ZONDERVAN

Scripture taken from the King James Version of the Bible.

WestBow Press books may be ordered through
booksellers or by contacting:

WestBow Press
A Division of Thomas Nelson & Zondervan
1663 Liberty Drive
Bloomington, IN 47403
www.westbowpress.com
1 (866) 928-1240

ISBN: 978-1-5127-5948-8 (sc)
ISBN: 978-1-5127-5949-5 (e)

Library of Congress Control Number: 2016916604

Print information available on the last page.

WestBow Press rev. date: 10/7/2016

Dedicated to

God the Father,
Jesus the Son,
and the Holy Spirit
and also
my children
Rick Whitaker,
Rod Whitaker, and
Debbie Whitaker Roberts;
their father,
Luther Whitaker;
their step-fathers,
Earl Lease and
Robert Walters;
and all my
grandchildren, great-grandchildren,
and
extended family.

Contents

Foreword 1

I am honored to express my feelings and opinions about Judy. I have known her for over forty years and have been married to her daughter, Debbie, for thirty years.

Over these years I have seen her go through many trying times in her life. I've seen her on the mountain and in the valley. However, I have never seen her give up. She is a fighter and a woman who fights for what she believes in. She has always kept her faith in God and held to his hand during those times she has spent in the valley. She has much life experience, and I know this book will be an encouragement to those who read it. I hold Judy in high esteem because she has always enriched the lives of those she has contact with, and I believe you will be blessed by this book.

Pastor Kenneth Roberts
Ashtabula Pentecostal Church of God
Ashtabula, Ohio

Foreword 2

Out of Darkness, into the Light is a short story about the life of Judy Ann Walters. Her life has been one with a lot of ups and downs, but through it she has learned to trust in Jesus Christ and the finished work of the cross.

I have had the privilege of knowing Judy most of my life and now have the privilege of working with her to reach souls for Christ. She truly has a heart to reach those who are lost. I have had the privilege of being her pastor for the past five years. She also sings in our worship team and is used of God in many different areas. I look forward to working with her till the coming of Jesus Christ to receive his body, the church. God bless.

Pastor Ronnie L. Patrick
New Beginnings Church and World Outreach
Warsaw, Indiana

Preface

This book is written to encourage people who are going through trials in their lives that God is faithful. It is also for people who do not know the Lord, to show how God works in people's lives and makes them overcomers if they keep their faith in him, no matter what they face. He is a great and merciful God who loves us beyond our comprehension. He made a way for us by giving his Son for us, that we will live with him for eternity. Praise God forever.

CHAPTER 1

Miracles Do Happen

My name is Judith Ann Clabaugh (Whitaker, Lease, Walters), and I was born on April 6, 1939, to Russel and Verda Rush Clabaugh. I was the eleventh child born out of twelve children. There were six girls and six boys.

My father worked on the Erie Railroad, and my mother worked in a factory in Huntington, Indiana. We were an average family, and I had hardworking parents who made a good living for the family.

When I was around four years old, some of the children got into an argument. My brother, who was two years older than me, and I went to tell my father about them arguing, since he worked just a couple of blocks from where we lived. We had to cross a street to get there, and my brother crossed the street before me and motioned for me to come across too. There was a taxicab coming down the street, and being a child, I couldn't judge distance, so I started out across the street. The car hit me and threw me up over the top of the hood. It knocked me out instantly, and I woke up in the doctor's office. That was one time the Lord saved me from death.

After my grandfather passed away when I was six years old, we moved from Huntington to our family farm in Etna Green, Indiana. By that time, there were only six of us children still at home. We grew a big garden and farmed the ground, which was only twenty acres. My dad continued working on the railroad, and he would drive to Rochester, Indiana, to get on the train.

The farmhouse was in bad shape, so my parents remodeled it and made it modern.

CHAPTER 2

Out of Darkness, into the Light

Eldest son Rick Whitaker and family

I started going to a church there in Etna Green, and when I was twelve years old, I went up front and got baptized in water—but there wasn't any change in my life. I didn't know that when you became a Christian, your life was supposed to become different. When I turned seventeen years old, I got pregnant out of wedlock. My parents were devastated, needless to say, and I was too. I thought my boyfriend wasn't going to marry me, so one night after we had been out, I came home and got my mother's sleeping pills. I made up my mind that I was going to take every pill that was in the bottle. I went to bed that night thinking I was going to get out of all my problems. The next morning my mom and dad found the empty pill bottle, and they found me and couldn't get me to wake up. They called the doctor, and he told them to pour coffee down my throat. They then took me over to my boyfriend's house; I didn't know anything about it because I was unconscious. His parents told them that he would marry me. The doctor said that if I would have taken two more pills, it would have killed me. Remember, I took all that were in the bottle. God had mercy on me and my baby. We were married on my husband's seventeenth birthday.

The following June, my baby was born—a

healthy baby boy. Thank God he was all right. Since my husband, Luther, was so young, it was hard for him to get a job, so we ended up on a farm in Rochester. He worked for a man who had a lot of farms. They furnished an old house for us to live in. We didn't make much money, but we made it somehow. During that time we had another child—another boy—and then we had a girl. Neither one of us were Christians. My husband's mother and father were Christians, and they started talking to me about the Bible. Because I had been baptized, I thought I was a Christian. At first I didn't like it because I thought they were saying I wasn't a Christian. But after a while, I started to read the Bible and saw that what they were telling me was true—I wasn't a Christian. I realized that if I died I would go to hell, and that made me feel miserable. Later on, my husband started having dreams where a hearse would back up to our door and start unloading caskets, small ones and larger ones. He was so tortured by these dreams that he didn't want to go to bed. One night he dreamed he had until June 11 to accept Jesus as his Savior.

In the dream he kept hearing a voice saying, "You better not put it off. You better not put it off."

Luther Whitaker

During this time, he was out in the field one day and a cow went berserk. It started chasing him, so he ran and jumped into the pickup truck. The cow ran into the pickup and smashed the door in. He thought this was it and that his time had come. He was so stubborn, but he went and got life insurance for the kids and me. But God has a way of working. One day toward the end of May, he told me that he would like to go to the church where he was raised and see some of the people he knew. So we went, and the Spirit of God moved him—he ran to the altar and received Jesus into his heart. I received Christ right after that. God changed our lives—we were born again. He told me afterward that he had no intention of getting saved—he just wanted to see some of the people he knew. But God had different plans. Praise the Lord.

We were then both baptized in water and received the infilling of the Holy Spirit. We couldn't wait to get to church, and when he would come home from work and after he ate his evening meal, he would get his Bible out and read and study the word. He was so hungry for God, and little did we know what God had in store for us.

CHAPTER 3

Miracles Do Happen More Than Once

The minister at the church was preaching on tithes, and like I said, we made very little money. But because the Bible says to pay tithes, we decided to try God. In Malachi 3:10, he said, "Try me, and see if I will not open the windows of heaven and pour you out a blessing that you cannot contain" (KJV). So we tried him, and my husband put a dollar in the offering. But then the following week he worried about it because we didn't have much money. Shortly after that, there was a farmer who had some ground across the road from where we lived. He raised potatoes. One day he asked me if he could use our phone, and when he came in the house, he set down a small bag of potatoes on the floor as a thank you. Because I let him use our phone, he brought a big, fifty-pound bag of potatoes for us. At that time, potatoes were very expensive. When my husband came home that night from work and saw that bag of potatoes, he knew that God had kept his promise—and from then on, we always paid tithes. And God always met our needs.

We lived there four years, and we bought our first house in Silver Lake, Indiana. Luther worked the night shift for about a year, and then our neighbor, who went to the same church as we did, asked him if he would like to work with him and learn the carpenter trade. So he started working with our neighbor, and in a very short time, Luther built the kitchen cabinets in our kitchen—and even before that, he built his mother's kitchen cabinets for her. He picked the carpentry trade right up, and before long he could do just about anything when it came to building.

During that time, I found out that I had cancer in my breast. I was twenty-six years old at the time. I was watching Oral Roberts one day, and he prayed for people on his program.

I put one of my hands on my breast where the cancer was, and I prayed with him. A couple of weeks later, an evangelist came to our church, and God directed him to me. He told me that it was a black cancer, which is melanoma, and that it really would have been bad—but that God was going to heal me. He prayed for me, but I couldn't tell that anything had changed. The following day, I was so discouraged; I thought that God showed me and my condition to him but that I didn't have enough faith to be healed. When my husband came home that evening, I told him about how I was feeling.

He said, "I can't believe anything but that you're healed."

When he said that, my faith came back to me. After he prayed for me, my cancer hurt me more than it ever had. The minister was holding a revival for us the next night, and I felt the Holy Spirit come in there where the cancer was. It felt soothing, and I also felt a sensation like the cancer was being lifted out of my body. And that was it—it was gone. Praise God. That's been fifty years ago, and I'm still healed. When God does something, he does it right.

One note I would like to make, God doesn't do things the same way. He healed me in this specific way, but he might heal someone else with the same illness in a different way. We can't put God in a box. You have to leave it to him, how he chooses to answer your prayer.

CHAPTER 4

Tried as If by Fire

When my husband was twenty-nine years old, he noticed that he was having some problems defecating. He went to the doctor and told the doctor his symptoms. The doctor didn't examine him and instead he just told Luther that it was probably his nerves from the kind of work he did. The doctor ended up just giving him some medicine to take. He took the medicine a couple of times, but then he quit taking it—he couldn't tell any difference. Several years later, he started having problems again, so he went to the doctor again. It was a different doctor this time, and he examined Luther and said that he had a cancer in his bowel. They did surgery on him and removed it, but to make sure, they wanted to give him radiation. However, he wouldn't take it because so many people had told him that it burns you really bad. He let it go, and a few years later, he started having problems again. He went back to the doctor, and they checked him and said he had a large cancer in his bowel. Through the years, we had seen God move in our lives and do miracles, so we decided to leave it in God's hands. We decided to go to Ernest Angely's church in Dayton, Ohio, and have him pray for him. All the way there, he couldn't hardly sit and was in a lot of pain, but Brother Angely, prayed for him, and all the pain left. We drove back to Indiana that night. He was fine, but he kept bleeding, so he went to the doctor, and they said it had shrunk to the size of a quarter. They wanted to do surgery and take the rest of it out. He was undecided about what to do, so he had the surgery and they took the rest of it out. They wanted to give him radiation, but he wouldn't take it. He seemed to be all right until he was forty-four years old.

CHAPTER 5

What an Opportunity to Spread the Gospel

When my husband was forty-two years old, one day he come to me and said, "Honey, I feel like the Lord is speaking to me to go on TV."

I said, "That's funny—I have been thinking the same thing."

Before that, the Lord had called him into the ministry. He said he didn't think they would let him on TV because he hadn't gone to Bible college, but we went to the TV station and asked them about us going on TV. We said that he hadn't been to Bible college.

They said, "That is just what we are looking for, someone who won't go over the people's heads."

That took that excuse away. Next he hadn't

told hardly anyone that he was thinking about going on TV, but one day shortly after that, a man walked up to him and said, "I hear you are thinking about going on TV. Here is a check for it."

It was a hundred dollars, so that was a confirmation to us that we were supposed to do this. In 1982, we went on TV, with our children and extended family members, on Sunday morning at 7:00 a.m. for a half-hour program. Our family did the singing, and my husband did the teaching. It wasn't long before they were running us free on Sunday morning and running us on Wednesday nights, prime time at 8:30. My husband said as long as the Lord provided the finances for the programs we would stay on. At times it didn't look like the money was going to be there, but it always was. We ended up on three different TV stations, South Bend, Indianapolis, and Richmond, Indiana. We were on South Bend for four and a half years. The name of the program was, "Voice of Truth."

During that time, my husband's cancer got worse, but he still went on doing what God had called him to do in spite of it. One

Sunday afternoon, he told me that he thought the Lord had spoken to him and wanted him to go to Tulsa, Oklahoma, to a Christian and prayer-based hospital that was there. I was the only one he had told that to. That night we went back to church, and one of the elders of the church came up to me and said they wanted to talk to my husband after church. They told my husband that they felt like he should go out to that hospital in Tulsa, and that if he would, they would pay his way out there. Well, that was a confirmation that we were supposed to go. We had no medical insurance because we couldn't afford it. We were only making $125 a week before taxes. We left for Tulsa, and when we got out there, we took his medical records with us, but they wanted to do their own tests.

They checked him out thoroughly and said he had cancer of the colon and rectum and that he should have been dead two years before that. Another miracle. They gave him six weeks of radiation. We were out there for three and a half months. While we were out there, they were running reruns of the TV outreach because he wasn't there to make any new ones. He didn't like that, but he felt that we didn't have enough money in the ministry to fly back home and make more programs. A day or two later, we got a check for $5,000 from one contributor for the broadcast. We flew back and made four programs and went back out to Tulsa and finished his radiation. We came back home then, and we were just there for a day or two. He started bleeding really heavy, so we had to leave and go right back out to Tulsa. The day we were leaving to go back, my husband had lost so much blood that he could hardly walk across the floor. He sat down to put his shoes on, and the Lord spoke to him and told him that he wanted him to put an outreach center in our church to help the poor and needy. Now remember he was so weak he couldn't hardly walk. He told the Lord if he would give him the strength, when we got back home he would. We went back to Tulsa, and they did major surgery. During that time, I was able to stay in the room with him and help take care of him.

CHAPTER 6

The Prayer Partner

Just about every day, one lady would come in and pray for him. She was his prayer partner. We had been doing adult Sunday school, TV ministry, street ministry, and jail ministry. She didn't know we were doing these ministries. One day she came in to pray for him, and she told him that God had another ministry for him to do. He didn't say anything to her about the ministry God had spoken to him about starting. The next day she came in and started singing a song about taking care of the poor. That was his confirmation that he was supposed to put the outreach center in. We saw God work in so many ways while we were there. He met all of our needs. It was fun watching him work. One day I went out into one of the lobbies they had there, and there was a minister sitting on the couch. We got to talking, and he told me his wife had been in the hospital there. When he went to check her out of the hospital, they found out he was a minister, and they asked him for his ministerial license. They made a copy of it and told him the bill was all taken care of. Talk about a God-appointed time. I went and told my husband what he told me, and when we went to check out, they took his ministerial license made a copy of it and said it was all taken care of. Remember when I said God spoke to him to go to that particular hospital. That was a miracle. That has been almost thirty-two years ago, and I would have still been paying on that bill if they hadn't taken care of it, but God is faithful.

CHAPTER 7

The Outreach Center

When we got back from Tulsa, my husband started putting the outreach center in right away. Our church had built a gymnasium for our Christian school, and down at one end of it there was a space over the shower rooms and bathrooms where there wasn't anything. This was on the second level. My husband asked the church if it would be all right if he put an outreach center up there, and they said it was. Remember I said we had no money during that time and no medical insurance. About a year before that, my father had passed away and left me an inheritance. We took that money and put in the outreach center. My husband and some others did the work and accomplished what God had told him to do. He got to work in the outreach center for a couple of years and was a blessing to a lot of people. During that time, we were still doing the TV ministry, street ministry, and jail ministry. He was a man of faith. James 2:17–18 says, "Even so Faith, if it has not works, is dead, being alone. Yes, a man may say, you have faith, and I have works, show me your faith without your works, and I will show you my faith by my works" (KJV). Even though he was still sick, he kept on doing ministry, by the grace of God. I never have seen anyone like him. He didn't give into his sickness and quit trying. I saw him go pray for sick people in the hospital who weren't nearly as sick as him. He would think to himself that he didn't know if he could make it up the steps, but he did. He would get back home and collapse. Two years after he put the outreach center in, he had to give up the ministry. He was so weak that he couldn't do anything. This was hard for him, because he was the type person who it seemed there wasn't anything he couldn't do. He was bedfast for six months. During that time, people would come to visit him and try to comfort him, but they would leave, encouraged themselves. He got to the place where he wanted to go on and be with the Lord, but we kept holding on to him. Then finally the night before he died, I told the Lord that if he wasn't going to heal him, I'd just as soon he would go ahead and take him. He died the next morning at 4:35 a.m., on September 5, 1987. We had been married thirty-two and a half years. Sometimes we are selfish with our loved ones because we want to keep them here with us, but God doesn't make any mistakes, and he knows what is best.

CHAPTER 8

Being Alone

Earl and Mary Lease

About a year before my husband passed away,
we had sold our large house that we had built

with our own money and moved into about a thousand square foot house. I had most of our married life been a stay-at-home mom and took care of the books when we were in the construction business and TV ministry. So, when my husband passed away, I had no life insurance and no work skills. I had no idea what I was going to do. I was working the outreach center and that was all. One day the principal of our Christian school asked me if I would like to fix the school lunches for the students, and I told him I would. I started doing that and the outreach center and made a little income, which supplemented me. Remember that I said we always paid our tithes. God took care of me, even though I didn't have much income. I had no life insurance or medical insurance. He met my needs. I believe if you pay your tithes, he will make a way for you, because he said he would in his word. If you don't pay your tithes, you don't have that promise. I'm not saying God won't take care of you; you just don't have that promise to lean on. I did the lunches and outreach center for two years after my husband passed away. God works in mysterious ways. After two years, all at once I got very lonely. I would walk up and down the streets and cry from loneliness. My brother-in-law—at the time I didn't know this—was planning on getting his cousin's husband and me together. She had passed away, and her name was Mary. I started thinking about him, and one night I was so lonely, I called him and talked to him for a while and that was it. A little bit after, he called me and asked me if he could come and take me out to supper the next night. I told him yes. He came the next night. He lived in Ohio, and we went out and really enjoyed each other's company. My husband and I used to go and see his wife and him when she was sick. I knew he was a very nice and good man. To make a short story shorter, we were married thirteen days after our first date. Ordinarily, I wouldn't have done that, but I prayed about it and believed it was God's will. He didn't want to live in Indiana, so I sold my home and moved to Ohio to live. We were very happy. I believe God has a plan for each one of our lives. Sometimes it is not easy. During my new husband's wife's sickness, he got bitter at God, and after she died, he was contemplating killing himself. Just a few nights later is when I called him. I believe God had his hand in this. After we got married, he turned around and got back with God. Like I said, we were very happy. We were doing ministry, and everything seemed to be going good. He had been having some problems with his back, so he went to a chiropractor. He was supposed to go back the following week for more treatments. That weekend we went to church. It was cold and snowy out. During Sunday school, I made the comment that my first husband had said to me when we were going through his illness, *"It doesn't matter what happens to us, just so God gets glory out of our lives"* Little did I know in just a few minutes I would be living that again. During the church service, he was really enjoying the service. He took off his suit jacket and handed it to me, and then in a little bit he took off his tie and handed it to me, and then all of a sudden, he got up and went back to the pastor's study. He motioned for his brother-in-law to come back with him. Then I heard them praying, and I thought he would be all right in a little bit. Then someone came out and told me Earl wanted to go home because he was sick. I got up and went back to get his coat. He had hung it in a different place than where I thought and I couldn't find it, so I gave up on that and went into the study where he was, and he wasn't talking anymore. In just a few minutes he was gone. He had a massive heart attack. I was in shock, like I was numb.

They said the last words he said were, "Lord, if you're ready to take me home, I'm ready to go."

We were only married for three months and three and a half days, and he was gone. Here I had sold my home and moved to Ohio, and now I had to face this. I was so confused. I thought I had missed God and that was why this had happened. I thought maybe I wasn't supposed to leave the outreach center, but when I prayed about it, I felt like it was okay for me to leave it and I had someone else to take my place. The morning after he passed away, and I woke up, "Because He Lives, I Can Face Tomorrow" was going over and over inside of me. That was the Holy Spirit comforting me. My daughter came and stayed with me through the funeral and the week after. My daughter and I went to midweek service that week, and I was sitting there with all these thoughts going through my mind, wondering if I had missed God. In my mind I was praying, and I said, "God, you just have to give me something." And I no more than prayed that in my mind that this sister in the church came up to me and started speaking in tongues. This is one of the nine spiritual gifts found in 1 Corinthians 12:7–11 (KJV). Then she interpreted in English what she said in tongues, and she said, "My daughter, I have ordained your footsteps, and again my daughter, I have ordained your footsteps." She said some other things that I don't remember. God in his goodness was letting me know that I hadn't missed him, that I was right where he wanted me. I believe that God put Earl and me together because Earl was backsliding, to get him back to him, because he knew Earl didn't have very long to live. God is so merciful. All the things I went through were worth it, if they caused Earl to come back to God. I know some people don't believe that a Christian can backslide. There are too many scriptures in the Bible that state that a Christian can backslide. God gave us a will, and he will not violate our will.

CHAPTER 9

Here We Go Again

Debbie and Ken Roberts with family

After Earl passed away, I had to move out of his house. We had an agreement that what was his went to his kids, and rightly so. After a length of time, I moved out into an apartment about twelve miles from there and got a job at a college, waiting tables. They wanted me to work Sundays and I didn't get to go to church, so I saw that wasn't going to work. After about three months, I moved back to Warsaw, Indiana, and rented an apartment. About a year after Earl died, I went to church one night, and a phone call came in. It was for me. My daughter, Debbie, was in intensive care in the Cleveland Clinic. They didn't know if she would make it or not. I left church immediately and went to the hospital, which was almost three hundred miles away. Her kidneys had quit working, her blood pressure had dropped way down, and she said she felt like she was on fire. They finally were able to get her blood pressure up some. She was in intensive care for five days and in the hospital three weeks. She came home and had to go back for another four days. I was there for two months taking care of her, and after it was all over, she asked the doctor what chance she had of making it, and he told her she had no chance. People all over were praying for her, and that is what saved her. Thank you, Jesus. She had toxic blood poisoning.

After two months, I had to leave her and go to Indianapolis, Indiana. My granddaughter, Teri, had pneumonia and was in an iron lung. She pulled through and was in the iron lung for a long period of time

Rod Whitaker and family

She was born with a birth deformity called spinal muscular atrophy, a form of MD. Her brain doesn't send the messages through the nerves to the muscles. She was diagnosed when she was about a year old, and they said she would probably only live another year. At this writing she is thirty-six years old. She has very little strength in her muscles to move or even hold her head up.

In 1988, when she was eight years old she had surgery for curvature of the spine. She recovered from that and went on to graduate from high school, and then she enrolled at IPFW in Fort Wayne, Indiana. Some of her cousins were going to that college too, so they looked after her, and when they graduated, she didn't have anyone to take care of her, so she had to leave college and went back home and lived with her parents. She was so disappointed to have to quit college. A couple of years after that she had some cousins who lived in Ohio and were going to Toledo University, and they told her if she wanted to go to college there that they would take care of her. She was so excited, but because she lived in another state, she would have to pay a higher tuition to go there, so she couldn't go there. But because of that she checked on Ball State College in Indiana, and they had services for disabled students. That would give them resources to provide for her care. She went there and got a degree in social work. She was so proud of herself, which she had a right to be. Later on she started having pain in her back, and her parents, Rod and Vicki, took her to the doctor. They said she would probably have to have surgery on her back and fuse her back together. They said it would really be a bad surgery. In the meantime her parents took her to church and had her prayed for. They noticed she wasn't complaining about her back hurting anymore. They took her back to the doctor, and they checked her and said that her back had fused together and said they couldn't have done that good of a job on it. She wouldn't have to have surgery. Isn't God good? She is very independent, and she moved to Indianapolis, Indiana, and got a job and bought a new home. We are so proud of her. When most people would have given up, she pushed forward and accomplished things that a lot of people with good health never accomplish.

CHAPTER 10

Joining the Work Force

Author with husband Bob Walters

I was living in the apartment for about six years and was working at a retail store. One day I decided I was tired of paying rent and it kept going up, so I bought a mobile home in a mobile home park. I lived there about three years. I had prayed about the Lord finding me someone I could share my life with again. There was a man across the street from me, and he asked me out. His name was Bob Walters. We dated for about a year and decided to get married. At the time I was going to the church that my first husband and I were going to. He hadn't been used to going to a full gospel church but started going with me to my church. He accepted our beliefs, and the Lord started to manifest himself to him. He had an uncle who had gotten cancer, and he needed someone to take him to Fort Wayne for radiation treatments. This happened before we got married. He had taken him to Fort Wayne for thirty radiation treatments before, but the cancer had come back and he needed thirty more treatments. He took his uncle one time, and his back started hurting him.

I came over to his house. Like I said, he lived just across the street from me. He was lying on the floor in a lot of pain. He told me he didn't know what he was going to do. He didn't think he would be able to take his uncle for his treatments. We said a simple little prayer together, and instantly he was healed. He said he felt heat go down his backbone, and the pain left instantly. The doctors had told him he had three bone spurs on his spine, and if you know anything about that, it is very painful. But God healed him in an instant. He was able then to finish taking his uncle for his radiation treatments. That's been about eighteen years ago at this writing, and he still hasn't had any problems with it. God is good all the time. About a year later we were married and at this writing have been married seventeen years. He is a very good man and is very good to me. He tries to please me in any way he can. We go to church and worship the Lord together and are waiting for the Lord's coming.

CHAPTER 11

The Great Revelation

Even though I had been a Christian since I was twenty years old and God had blessed me in so many ways, I didn't understand about the cross of Christ and what Jesus had done for me. I had been taught the law, where you lived a holy life by your own willpower and efforts. I failed all the time and kept getting worse instead of better. I lived under condemnation and fear all the time. I was trusting in myself and what I thought I could do, instead of trusting in Christ and what he did for me. I lived that way for forty-seven years and was miserable. I was born again, so I wanted to live right but didn't know how to. Most people would have given up, but I knew I couldn't. My soul was at stake. I just kept trying to live a Christian life in my own strength. When I had come to the end of my rope and knew I couldn't do it, the light came on, and I finally saw what Jesus had done for me. I couldn't add anything to that; he had done it all. What a load that took off of me when he gave me the revelation of the cross. I was like the apostle Paul, in Romans 7:15 (KJV) when he talked about when he wanted to do good, he did evil and couldn't find the power to do the good that he wanted to do. But when he got the revelation of the cross, he said in Romans 8:1 (KJV), "There is therefore now no condemnation to them who are in Christ Jesus, who walk not after the flesh, but after the Spirit." When you try to live the Christian life in your own power and strength, you are walking in your flesh. God said our righteousness is as filthy rags. He will only accept the righteousness we accept by faith by what Jesus did for us. That is when we enter into his rest that he talks about. Praise his name. I want to praise him through eternity for what he has done for me. I believe there are many people who don't understand about the cross. They walk around defeated and in fear all the time. Like I said before, that is a miserable existence. But thank God, I finally got that revelation, and I want to praise Jesus through eternity for what he has done for me. I could never thank him enough, and he deserves all the praise and glory, forever.

CHAPTER 12

Being Caught Up (Rapture of the Church)

Mathew 24:36 (KJV) says, "But of that day and hour knows no man, no, not the Angels in heaven, but My Father only." There have been people and ministers down through the years who have predicted exactly when they thought the rapture was going to take place, but as you can see, they were wrong. No man, even Jesus, knows the day or the hour, but the Father only. The Bible gives us signs that we can know that it is near, at the door, but we don't know exactly when. He told us to be ready, for at any time he can come. He said some would say he delayed his coming. Luke 12:45 (KJV) says, "He told us to look up, for our redemption draweth nigh," and he is coming after those that are looking for him and love his appearing. Second Timothy 4:8 (KJV) says, "Even so come quickly, Lord Jesus, come quickly."

CHAPTER 13

Salvation by Faith

If you haven't received Jesus as your Personal Savior, I invite you to do so now. The Bible says in 2 Corinthians 6:2, "Behold, now is the acceptable time, behold, now is the day of salvation" (KJV).

We have no promise of tomorrow. Jesus paid such a great price for our salvation, and he wants everyone to be saved and have eternal life. He said, unless we are born again, we cannot see the kingdom of heaven. When we accept him by sincerely repenting of our sins, we *are born again (John 3:3, 5–7 KJV)*, and he changes our hearts. The things that we once loved, we will hate (that's talking about sin), and the things that we once hated (righteousness), we will then love. We will want to please Jesus then. After you receive him, be baptized in water. Ask God to lead you to a good church that worships Jesus in Spirit and in truth, for the Bible says in John 4:23, "He seeketh such to worship him in Spirit and in truth" (KJV). Get into his word, and see all the promises he has promised you. The Bible says in 2 Timothy 2:15, "Study to show yourself approved, a workman that needeth not to be ashamed, rightly dividing the word of truth" (KJV). James 4:8 says, "Draw near to Jesus and he will draw near to you" (KJV). Pray every day. You don't do these things to earn your salvation. Jesus gave you your salvation as a gift. You can do nothing to add to what he done for you. Doing these things helps you to get closer to him and have fellowship with him. He loves us so much and just requires us to have faith in what he done for us. That makes us perfect in the eyes of God. Even though we cannot be perfect, he accepts what Jesus did for us, and that makes us perfect in God's eyes. After we become Christians, there are times when we are going to sin, and we need to ask God for forgiveness. He said he would forgive us if we sincerely ask him to (1 John 1:9 KJV). We don't live a lifestyle of sin, but at times we will sin. We are more apt to sin if we aren't spending time with God like we should and fellowshipping with him.

God is so good, and his mercy endures forever. May this book be a blessing to you and build your faith in God. To God be all the glory. Amen.

Rod and Vicki Whitaker with grandchildren

Rick Whitaker and grandson

Jonathan and Joshua Roberts

Author and family

Debbie and Ken Roberts with children